EASTER
COLORING BOOK
FOR KIDS AGES 2-5

SEFONT

BETTER LIFE, ONE PAGE AT A TIME

EASTER
COLORING BOOK
FOR KIDS AGES 2-5

THIS BOOK BELONGS TO:

EASTER
COLORING BOOK
FOR KIDS AGES 2-5

EASTER
COLORING BOOK
FOR KIDS AGES 2-5

EASTER
COLORING BOOK
FOR KIDS AGES 2-5

EASTER
COLORING BOOK
FOR KIDS AGES 2-5

EASTER
COLORING BOOK
FOR KIDS AGES 2-5

EASTER

COLORING BOOK

FOR KIDS AGES 2-5

EASTER
COLORING BOOK
FOR KIDS AGES 2-5

EASTER
COLORING BOOK
FOR KIDS AGES 2-5

EASTER
COLORING BOOK
FOR KIDS AGES 2-5

EASTER
COLORING BOOK
FOR KIDS AGES 2-5

EASTER

COLORING BOOK

FOR KIDS AGES 2-5

EASTER
COLORING BOOK
FOR KIDS AGES 2-5

EASTER
COLORING BOOK
FOR KIDS AGES 2-5

EASTER
COLORING BOOK
FOR KIDS AGES 2-5

EASTER
COLORING BOOK
FOR KIDS AGES 2-5

EASTER

COLORING BOOK

FOR KIDS AGES 2-5

EASTER
COLORING BOOK
FOR KIDS AGES 2-5

EASTER
COLORING BOOK
FOR KIDS AGES 2-5

EASTER

COLORING BOOK

FOR KIDS AGES 2-5

EASTER
COLORING BOOK
FOR KIDS AGES 2-5

EASTER
COLORING BOOK
FOR KIDS AGES 2-5

EASTER
COLORING BOOK
FOR KIDS AGES 2-5

EASTER
COLORING BOOK
FOR KIDS AGES 2-5

EASTER
COLORING BOOK
FOR KIDS AGES 2-5

EASTER
COLORING BOOK
FOR KIDS AGES 2-5

EASTER
COLORING BOOK
FOR KIDS AGES 2-5

EASTER
COLORING BOOK
FOR KIDS AGES 2-5

EASTER
COLORING BOOK
FOR KIDS AGES 2-5

EASTER
COLORING BOOK
FOR KIDS AGES 2-5

EASTER
COLORING BOOK
FOR KIDS AGES 2-5

EASTER
COLORING BOOK
FOR KIDS AGES 2-5

EASTER
COLORING BOOK
FOR KIDS AGES 2-5

EASTER
COLORING BOOK
FOR KIDS AGES 2-5

EASTER
COLORING BOOK
FOR KIDS AGES 2-5

EASTER
COLORING BOOK
FOR KIDS AGES 2-5

EASTER
COLORING BOOK
FOR KIDS AGES 2-5

EASTER
COLORING BOOK
FOR KIDS AGES 2-5

EASTER
COLORING BOOK
FOR KIDS AGES 2-5

EASTER

COLORING BOOK

FOR KIDS AGES 2-5

Made in the USA
Las Vegas, NV
29 March 2024